ULTIMATE STICKER COLLECTION
CHOOSE YOUR SIDE!

How to use this book

Read the captions, then find the sticker that best fits the space. (Hint: check the sticker labels for clues!)

•

Don't forget that your stickers can be stuck down and peeled off again.

•

There are lots of fantastic extra stickers for creating your own scenes throughout the book.

LONDON, NEW YORK,
MELBOURNE, MUNICH, AND DELHI

Written by Shari Last
Edited by Garima Sharma
Designed by Lauren Rosier and Suzena Sengupta
Jacket designed by Suzena Sengupta
DTP Designer Umesh Singh Rawat

First published in the United States in 2014
by DK Publishing,
345 Hudson Street, New York, New York 10014

14 15 16 17 10 9 8 7 6 5 4 3 2
002–187818–May/14

A CIP catalog record for this book is available from the Library of Con..... .

ISBN: 978-1-4654-1985-9

Color repro....
Printed and bound .....

Di....
ww....
www....

TWO SIDES OF THE FORCE

The galaxy is in crisis. The peaceful Republic is under threat from corrupt Separatists, who do not want to live under Republic rule. The noble Jedi use the light side of the Force to defend the Republic. But the evil Sith have chosen the dangerous dark side of the Force—and they want to take control of the galaxy forever.

THE JEDI

The Jedi are powerful warriors who use the light side of the Force. They long for peace, but are prepared to battle against evil.

PALPATINE

Chancellor Palpatine is the leader of the Republic. He pretends to want a peaceful galaxy, but he hides a very dark secret...

DARTH SIDIOUS

The evil Sith study the dark side of the Force. Darth Sidious is the Sith leader, but nobody knows he is Chancellor Palpatine in disguise.

DARTH MAUL

Darth Maul is a Sith. His body was cut in half by Jedi Obi-Wan Kenobi, so he walks on robotic legs. Now, Maul wants revenge!

COUNT DOOKU

Count Dooku used to be a Jedi, but he has turned to the dark side. Now, he leads the Separatists and commands the droid army.

GALAXY PATROL
This police gunship patrols the busy planet Coruscant—the capital of the Republic.

APPRENTICES
Count Dooku trained Asajj Ventress and Savage Opress as his Sith apprentices. But will these dangerous creatures ever truly obey him?

JEK-14
Jek-14 is created by Count Dooku to be the most powerful Sith apprentice ever. But Jek-14 is not sure if he wants to be evil…

JEDI OR SITH?
Jedi Anakin Skywalker is not able to resist the power of the dark side. He will soon turn against the Jedi and battle Obi-Wan Kenobi.

RISE OF A SITH LORD
When Anakin is injured during his battle with Obi-Wan, he becomes Darth Vader—an evil Sith Lord kept alive by a mechanical suit and mask.

BATTLE OF NABOO

The evil Sith Lord Darth Sidious wants to control the galaxy. He secretly organizes an attack on the peaceful planet Naboo. On his orders, a massive droid army descends on the planet's grassy plains. The Gungan people of Naboo must decide whether to stand up and fight, or to surrender. Can they save their planet?

BATTLE DROID
Battle droids are controlled by the Separatists. They obey orders without question, but they cannot think for themselves.

MTT
There are thousands of battle droids in the Separatist droid army. How will they get to the battlefield? Easy—each Multi-Troop Transport (MTT) can carry 112 battle droids!

JAR JAR BINKS
Jar Jar is a clumsy Gungan—but he really wants to help defend his home planet. During the battle, Jar Jar destroys lots of battle droids.

AAT
The Armored Assault Tank (AAT) is a fearsome weapon. The droid army uses it to blast through everything in its way.

NABOO STARFIGHTER
Up in space, hundreds of yellow Naboo starfighters attack droid control ships. Can they defeat the droid army?

Use your extra stickers to create your own scene.

READY FOR BATTLE

The droid army expects to conquer Naboo with ease—but they are in for a surprise!

BATTLE OF GEONOSIS

The Separatists have built a secret battle droid factory on the planet Geonosis. When the Jedi find out, they lead the Republic army of clone troopers in an attack on the growing Separatist army. On the desert plains of Geonosis, the Clone Wars have begun!

CLONE TROOPER
The Jedi build an army of clones to help them take on the droid army. The clone troopers fight without fear.

COMMAND STATION
The clone command station is well equipped to help clone sergeants direct their troops straight from the battlefield.

AT-TE
The All Terrain Tactical Enforcer (AT-TE) is an enormous walking tank. It can carry 38 clone troopers onto a battlefield.

ALLIANCE TANK DROID
This dangerous droid can roll over any terrain, flattening everything in its path. Clone troopers—watch out!

BARC SPEEDER
Obi-Wan Kenobi chases battle droids in the superfast BARC speeder. Its sidecar can rotate to fire the blaster cannon in all directions!

DROIDEKA
The droideka is designed to destroy clone troopers. It has twin blasters and a powerful defense shield.

AT-RT
The powerful All Terrain Reconnaissance Transport (AT-RT) has a swiveling laser cannon to blast any battle droids who get in its way.

HOMING SPIDER DROID
The spider droid can blast its laser weapon at targets on the ground and in the air. It can even walk underwater and climb walls!

COMMANDO DROID CAPTAIN
Commando droid captains are built to be faster, stronger, and more intelligent than regular battle droids.

ARTILLERY CANNON
The clone army uses the artillery cannon to blast battle droids out of the way!

JEDI AT WAR

The Jedi are peacekeepers and prefer to avoid fighting, but they understand that sometimes there is no other option. During the Clone Wars, the brave Jedi swoop into battle aboard enormous Republic attack gunships. Enemies, beware!

SWOOP BIKE

Clone troopers use speedy swoop bikes to zip in and out of big battles.

OBI-WAN KENOBI

Obi-Wan keeps his cool in battle situations. He hates flying, but he happens to be an excellent pilot!

CLONE CAPTAIN

The clone trooper captain flies the Republic gunship. His ship can carry up to 30 clones.

COLEMAN TREBOR

Coleman is a Vurk, from the planet Sembla. He prefers negotiating to fighting, but is ready to wage war if he must.

SAESEE TIIN

Saesee Tiin has the ability to read minds. He uses this skill to his advantage in battles.

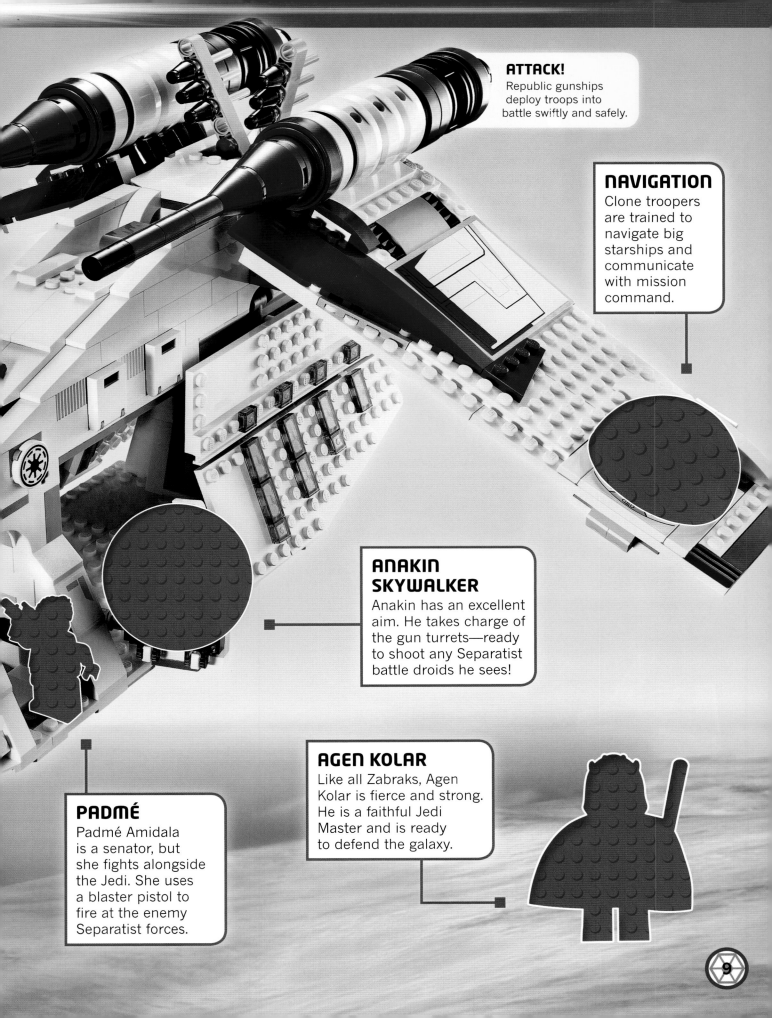

ATTACK!
Republic gunships deploy troops into battle swiftly and safely.

NAVIGATION
Clone troopers are trained to navigate big starships and communicate with mission command.

ANAKIN SKYWALKER
Anakin has an excellent aim. He takes charge of the gun turrets—ready to shoot any Separatist battle droids he sees!

AGEN KOLAR
Like all Zabraks, Agen Kolar is fierce and strong. He is a faithful Jedi Master and is ready to defend the galaxy.

PADMÉ
Padmé Amidala is a senator, but she fights alongside the Jedi. She uses a blaster pistol to fire at the enemy Separatist forces.

BATTLE OF CORUSCANT

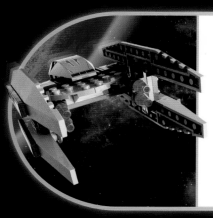

Chancellor Palpatine has been kidnapped! Obi-Wan Kenobi and Anakin Skywalker track him down aboard the starship of a droid army commander called General Grievous. As the Jedi fly through space above the planet Coruscant to rescue Palpatine, a huge battle rages between the Republic and Separatist fleets.

REPUBLIC ATTACK CRUISER

This huge ship carries hundreds of Republic starfighters into battle. It is also equipped with laser cannons and torpedo launchers.

VULTURE DROID

Vulture droids fly through space without a pilot. They receive commands from a droid control ship and attack the Republic fleet.

DROID TRI-FIGHTER

The extremely fast and accurate droid tri-fighters fly unpiloted, too. These droids strike fear in the hearts of Republic pilots.

V-WING PILOT

V-wing pilots train hard to fly their fast starfighters. They work together with an astromech droid to avoid enemy fire.

V-WING

The Republic V-wing starfighters are small and speedy. They can maneuver across a dangerous battlefield—and even escape droid tri-fighters!

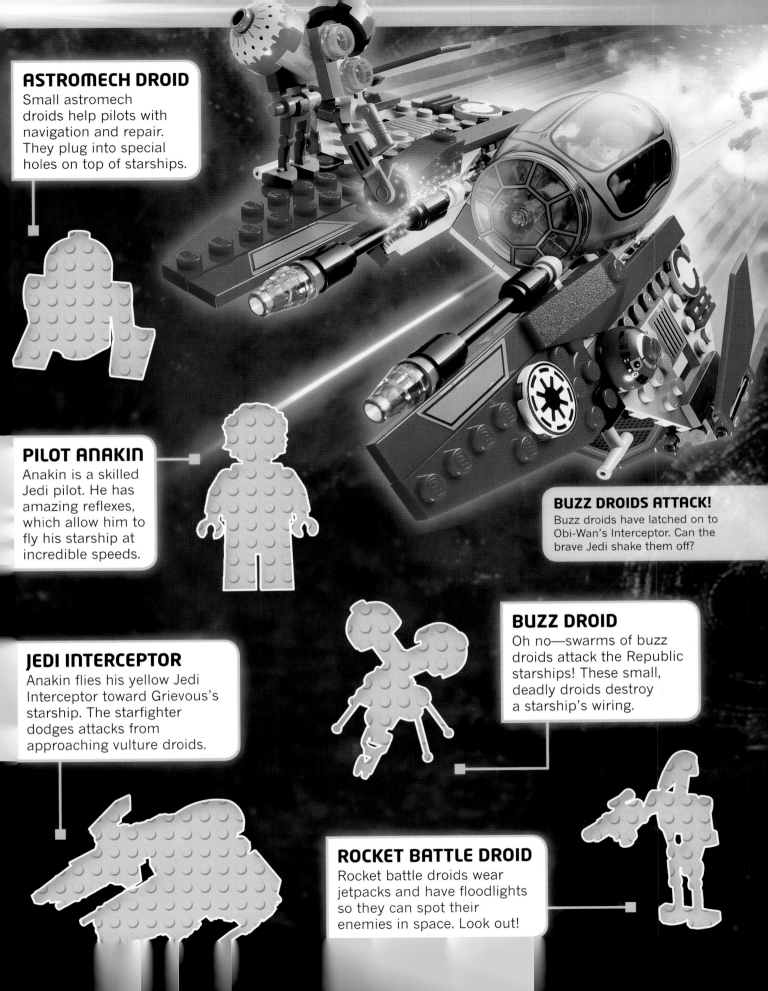

ASTROMECH DROID

Small astromech droids help pilots with navigation and repair. They plug into special holes on top of starships.

PILOT ANAKIN

Anakin is a skilled Jedi pilot. He has amazing reflexes, which allow him to fly his starship at incredible speeds.

BUZZ DROIDS ATTACK!

Buzz droids have latched on to Obi-Wan's Interceptor. Can the brave Jedi shake them off?

BUZZ DROID

Oh no—swarms of buzz droids attack the Republic starships! These small, deadly droids destroy a starship's wiring.

JEDI INTERCEPTOR

Anakin flies his yellow Jedi Interceptor toward Grievous's starship. The starfighter dodges attacks from approaching vulture droids.

ROCKET BATTLE DROID

Rocket battle droids wear jetpacks and have floodlights so they can spot their enemies in space. Look out!

BATTLE OF KASHYYYK

When the Separatists invade the planet Kashyyyk with their vast droid army, the clone troopers are worried. But the battle turns quickly when the native Wookiees decide to fight for their planet. Thanks to the Jedi's smart planning and Wookiees' brute strength, it seems that victory is within reach for the Republic.

CHIEF TARFFUL
Tarfful is the chief of a tribe of Wookiees. He is not a general, but he leads the Wookiee army to protect his home planet.

JEDI GENERALS
Jedi Generals Quinlan Vos and Luminara Unduli lead the clone troopers on Kashyyyk. They fight alongside the Wookiee army.

CATAMARAN
The Wookiees have many vehicles for traveling across their swampy planet. The catamaran is a fast, sturdy boat, which can also fly in the air!

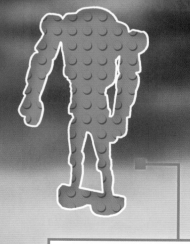

CHEWBACCA
Chewbacca is a brave soldier in the Wookiee army. He uses a powerful bowcaster to fire at the battle droids.

SUPER BATTLE DROID
These tall, scary droids are programmed to be fearless in battle. They shoot at their enemies with blasters built into their arms!

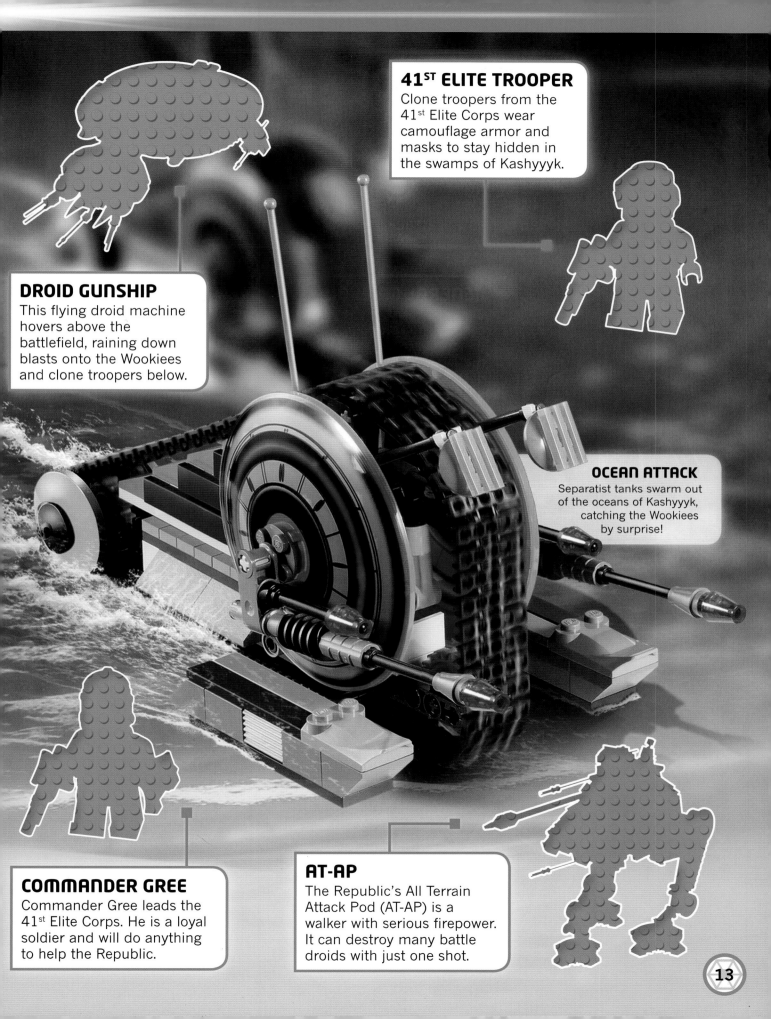

41ST ELITE TROOPER
Clone troopers from the 41st Elite Corps wear camouflage armor and masks to stay hidden in the swamps of Kashyyyk.

DROID GUNSHIP
This flying droid machine hovers above the battlefield, raining down blasts onto the Wookiees and clone troopers below.

OCEAN ATTACK
Separatist tanks swarm out of the oceans of Kashyyyk, catching the Wookiees by surprise!

COMMANDER GREE
Commander Gree leads the 41st Elite Corps. He is a loyal soldier and will do anything to help the Republic.

AT-AP
The Republic's All Terrain Attack Pod (AT-AP) is a walker with serious firepower. It can destroy many battle droids with just one shot.

BATTLE OF UTAPAU

The droid army has taken over the planet Utapau. General Grievous is plotting with the Separatist council, preparing to make his next move. Obi-Wan Kenobi soon arrives and confronts Grievous in a fierce lightsaber duel. Meanwhile, the Republic army launches an attack against the Separatist droids.

GENERAL GRIEVOUS

General Grievous is a cyborg who commands the droid army. He hates the Jedi and wants to destroy Obi-Wan.

GENERAL KENOBI

The Jedi General lands on Utapau with a battalion of clone troopers. He is determined not to let General Grievous escape.

MAGNAGUARDS

Grievous surrounds himself with droid bodyguards called MagnaGuards. They are strong, but Obi-Wan defeats them easily.

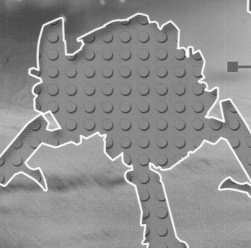

WHEEL BIKE

Grievous rides a speedy wheel bike. The bike has four clawed legs to climb up the steep cliffs of Utapau.

BOGA

Obi-Wan climbs onto a varactyl beast named Boga and chases Grievous when the general tries to escape on his wheel bike.

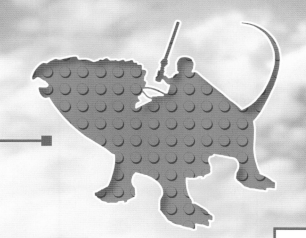

COMMANDER CODY

Commander Cody is Obi-Wan's second in command. He leads the 212th Attack Battalion into battle against the droid army.

HAILFIRE DROID

Hailfire droids unleash their many missiles against the clone army. With big wheels and missile launchers, they are a scary sight. Run!

OCTUPTARRA TRI-DROID

This skinny, three-legged droid can turn its head and fire lasers in any direction. It is not easy to destroy this droid.

INVADING FORCE

Droid soldiers patrol the planet Utapau. Can the clone troopers defeat them?

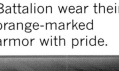

UTAPAU TROOPERS

Troopers from the 212th Attack Battalion wear their orange-marked armor with pride.

SIEGE OF SALEUCAMI

The Republic discovers top-secret Separatist cloning factories on the planet Saleucami. Jedi General Stass Allie and her team of clone troopers lead an attack against the factories, but they face tough resistance from the droid army. After a tense battle, the Jedi succeed in their mission.

SALEUCAMI TROOPER

The Republic's 91st Recon Corps patrol Saleucami. Troopers ride BARC speeders to travel over the crater-filled landscape.

STASS ALLIE

Stass Allie is a powerful healer. She prefers negotiation to war, but she knows that the Clone Wars could save the Republic.

STAP

Battle droids ride on Single Trooper Aerial Platforms (STAPs), which are equipped with dual blaster cannons.

SALEUCAMI CANNON

Battle droids hide their cannons in the reeds and shrubs of Saleucami. They wait for the Jedi and clone troopers to speed past.

AMBUSH

Watch out for hidden super battle droids! Their arm blasters are deadly.

BATTLE OF UMBARA

Umbara is a dark planet, home to lots of dangerous wildlife. When the Umbarans choose to join the Separatists, the clone army arrives to confront them. Led by Jedi General Pong Krell, the clone army is strong and fierce. But Krell is hiding a secret. How will this affect the battle?

PONG KRELL

With his four arms and two double-bladed lightsabers, Pong Krell is good to have on your team. But this Jedi Master is being drawn to the dark side...

501ST LEGION TROOPER

The 501st Legion follows Jedi General Pong Krell into battle. They don't realize that he is secretly trying to sabotage them.

MOBILE HEAVY CANNON

This Umbaran battle machine has a rotating cockpit and a missile launcher. Will the clone troopers find cover in time?

212TH CLONE TROOPER

Troopers from the 212th Attack Battalion swarm across the dangerous landscape of Umbara, searching for enemy traps.

UMBARAN SOLDIER

The soldiers of Umbara wear helmets that fill up with a special gas to improve their reflexes in battle.

TWO SIDES OF THE GALAXY

The Clone Wars ended after the heroic Jedi were defeated by the evil Sith. Now, Emperor Palpatine has taken control of the galaxy and turned it into an evil Sith Empire. However, a small group of rebels and one Jedi Knight are determined to destroy the Sith and bring peace and happiness back to the galaxy.

DARTH VADER
Darth Vader leads the Imperial Army of the evil Empire. He is feared by everyone in the galaxy—including his own soldiers!

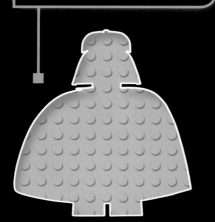

IMPERIAL OFFICER
Imperial officers work on the huge battle station, the Death Star. They operate the computers, fire the cannons, and help plan the Empire's next move.

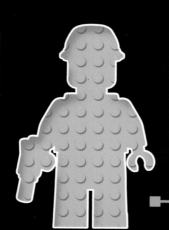

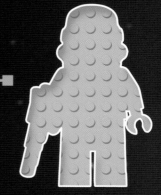

STORMTROOPER
All the soldiers of the Empire wear identical white armor and carry deadly blasters. Rebels, beware!

BOBA FETT
The most famous bounty hunter in the galaxy, Boba Fett is fast and fierce. He is hired by Darth Vader to capture Han Solo.

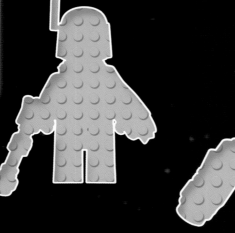

DEATH STAR GUNNER
Thousands of Death Star gunners are trained to defend the Death Star from rebel attacks.

LEIA

Princess Leia is a senator from Alderaan. She is on a mission to bring peace and justice to the galaxy.

LUKE SKYWALKER

Luke Skywalker is a Jedi Knight—and the secret son of Darth Vader. Will Luke choose the path of the light side or the dark side?

IMPERIAL MIGHT

The Empire uses huge Star Destroyer ships to travel the galaxy and enforce Imperial rule.

MON MOTHMA

Mon Mothma is one of the leaders of the Rebel Alliance. She will try her hardest to end the rule of the Empire.

LANDO CALRISSIAN

Gambler Lando Calrissian chooses to join the Rebel Alliance. He does not want the Empire to remain in control of the galaxy.

HAN SOLO

Han Solo is the pilot of the starship *Millennium Falcon*. He joins the rebels in many space battles, and helps them fight the Imperial Army.

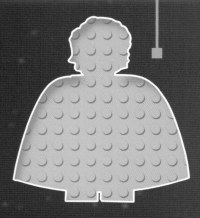

CAPTURED BY JABBA

Jabba the Hutt is a dangerous and powerful criminal who lives on the planet Tatooine. He often holds people captive until he gets what he wants. Jabba is not a Jedi or a Sith, but he joins forces with whichever side will benefit him the most. When Jabba captures Han Solo, he finds himself battling against the rebels.

MAX REBO
Max Rebo is the lead musician in the Max Rebo Band. The band is forced to play music for Jabba in exchange for food.

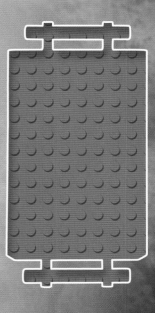

HAN IN CARBONITE
Han Solo causes Jabba so much trouble that the crime lord captures and freezes him in a substance called carbonite.

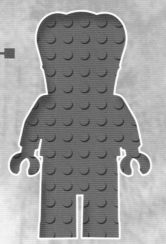

OOLA
Oola is a Twi'lek dancer. She thought dancing for Jabba would be a good job, but she was wrong! Now she can never leave.

PRINCESS LEIA
Princess Leia tries to rescue her friend Han Solo, but she is captured as well! Now Leia is chained to Jabba himself.

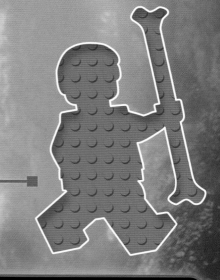

JEDI PRISONER
Jabba is excited because he has captured Luke Skywalker, a Jedi. But it is a trick—Luke wants to be caught so he can free Han and Leia.

Use your extra stickers to create your own scene.

RANCOR
This monster lives in a pit under Jabba's palace. Stay away—he is very dangerous!

BATTLE OF YAVIN

The Imperial Army has found the secret rebel base on the moon Yavin 4. The rebels must defend their base and destroy the Empire's deadly weapon, the Death Star. Rebel pilots soar through space in battle formation, but the Imperial fleet is in attack position, too. The battle is about to begin!

JEDI PILOT
Luke is an amazing pilot. He flies his X-wing along the surface of the Death Star, looking for the best spot to attack.

REBEL STARFIGHTER
X-wings are the best ships in the rebel fleet. They have four wings, four laser cannons, and a defense shield.

DEATH STAR
The Death Star is a moon-sized battle station, built by Emperor Palpatine.

VADER'S TIE FIGHTER
Darth Vader's TIE fighter is no ordinary starship. It has a strong hull and an accurate weapons targeting system.

PILOT VADER
Darth Vader flies his TIE fighter behind Luke's X-wing. Will Vader be able to match Luke's piloting skills?

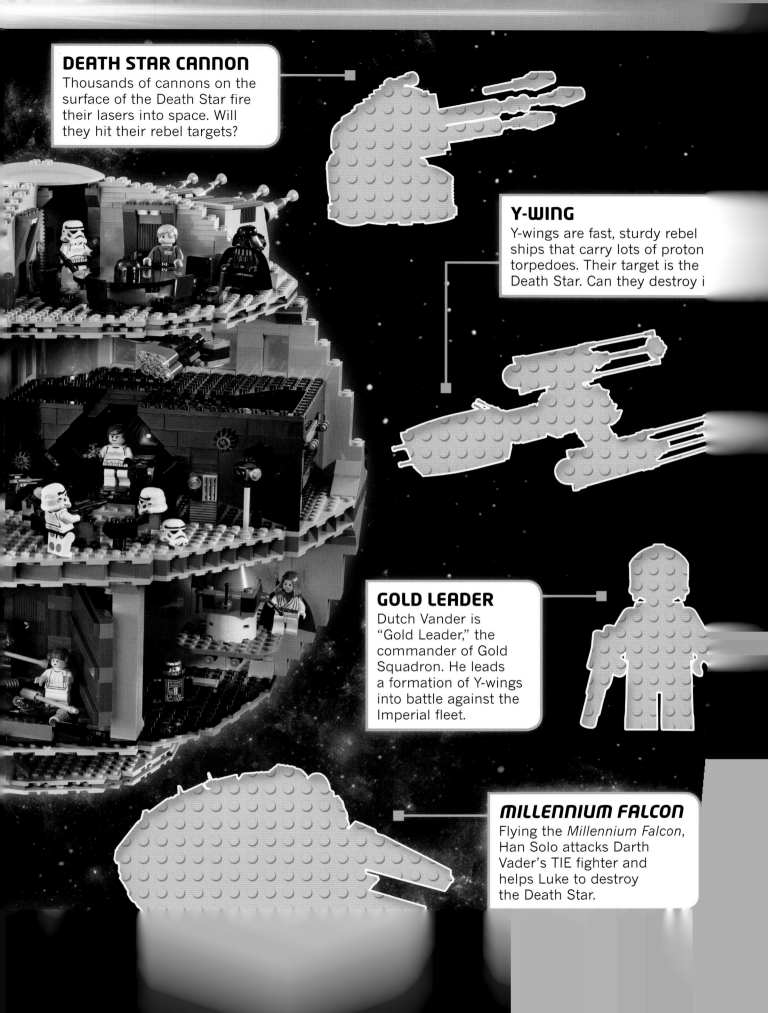

DEATH STAR CANNON
Thousands of cannons on the surface of the Death Star fire their lasers into space. Will they hit their rebel targets?

Y-WING
Y-wings are fast, sturdy rebel ships that carry lots of proton torpedoes. Their target is the Death Star. Can they destroy i

GOLD LEADER
Dutch Vander is "Gold Leader," the commander of Gold Squadron. He leads a formation of Y-wings into battle against the Imperial fleet.

MILLENNIUM FALCON
Flying the *Millennium Falcon*, Han Solo attacks Darth Vader's TIE fighter and helps Luke to destroy the Death Star.

BATTLE OF HOTH

Concealed on the barren, icy plains of the planet Hoth is Echo Base, the new headquarters of the Rebel Alliance. But it won't stay hidden for long. Darth Vader and his army are on their way to Hoth—and they are going to launch a devastating ground assault! Can the rebels defend their base?

PROBE DROID
Darth Vader sends probe droids to find out where the rebels are hiding. One of them tracks down the rebels on Hoth.

GENERAL VEERS
Imperial officer General Veers leads the attack on Echo Base. He is an expert on AT-AT walkers.

GENERAL RIEEKAN
General Rieekan is a clever rebel leader. He directs his troopers and helps them to avoid enemy fire.

P-TOWER TURRET
Blast away at the Imperial snowtroopers! The P-Tower turret swivels so it can fire powerful laser beams at approaching enemies.

SNOWTROOPERS
Vader's snowtroopers zip lightly over snow on their small, fast speeders. Watch out!

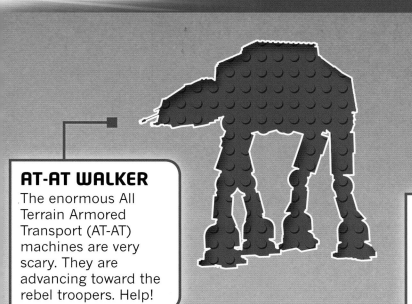

AT-AT WALKER
The enormous All Terrain Armored Transport (AT-AT) machines are very scary. They are advancing toward the rebel troopers. Help!

SNOWSPEEDER
There's only one way to defeat an AT-AT! Luke flies his snowspeeder around the huge walker's legs, tripping it up with a heavy cable.

HAN ON HOTH
Han Solo loves the warm sandy beaches of his home planet Corellia—he doesn't like the icy wastelands of Hoth. Brrr!

LEADER LEIA
Princess Leia plans battle strategies with rebel generals and officers at Echo Base.

READY, AIM, FIRE!
Rebel troopers on Hoth are ready to defend their base.

UNDERCOVER!

It looks like some of our heroes have decided to join forces with the Empire. But they have actually chosen the opposite! These brave adventurers are working undercover to rescue their friends from danger. They wear disguises to confuse their enemies. Will their cunning missions succeed?

STORMTROOPER LUKE
Has Luke joined the Imperial Army? No—he has disguised himself as a stormtrooper so he can enter the Death Star prison level undetected.

BOUSHH
Has Boushh the bounty hunter brought Jabba a prisoner? No—it's Princess Leia in disguise! She is on a mission to save Han Solo.

STORMTROOPER HAN
Han Solo also wears stormtrooper armor. He is helping Luke rescue Princess Leia from Darth Vader on the Death Star.

WOOKIEE PRISONER
Chewbacca hasn't really been captured... he's pretending to be handcuffed so he can enter Jabba's palace and save Han!

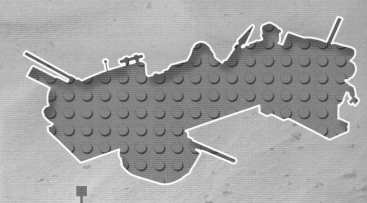

LANDO THE GUARD
Lando wears the uniform of one of Jabba's guards. But he's waiting to reveal his identity and save Luke.

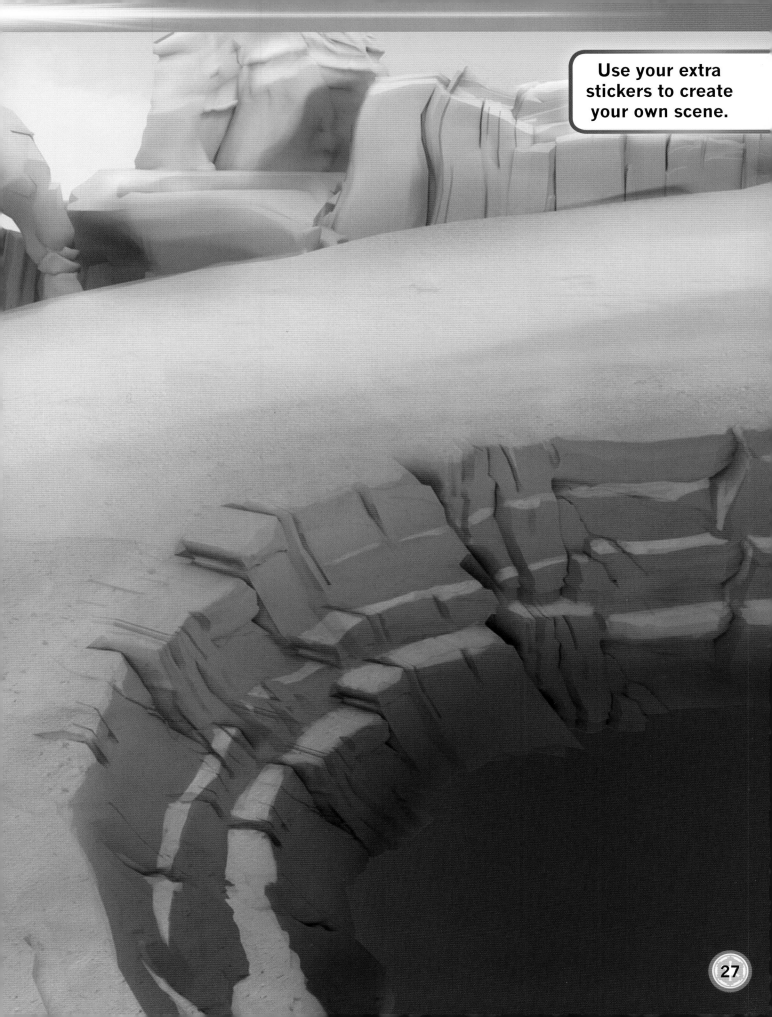

TREETOP ADVENTURE

Deep in the forests on the moon of Endor, a tribe of Ewoks live in a treetop village. Their quiet planet has been invaded by the Imperial Army and the rebels have arrived to confront them. The Ewoks have a choice: should they join the stormtroopers or the rebels?

LEIA ON ENDOR
Princess Leia is welcomed by the Ewok tribe. The Ewoks give her a dress made from materials from their village.

CAUGHT BY EWOKS
The Ewoks have made Luke their prisoner. Can he use the Force to persuade the small, furry warriors to help the rebels?

WICKET
Wicket is a friendly young Ewok. He meets Princess Leia in the forest and rescues her from a stormtrooper.

TREETOP VILLAGE
Ewoks build their villages in trees to protect them from intruders.

HAN IN DANGER
The Ewoks are going to roast Han Solo on a spit over the fire! How will Han get out of this tough spot?

IMPERIAL SPEEDER BIKE
Imperial stormtroopers patrol the forests of Endor. They ride super-fast speeder bikes, but the Ewoks have a plan to stop them.

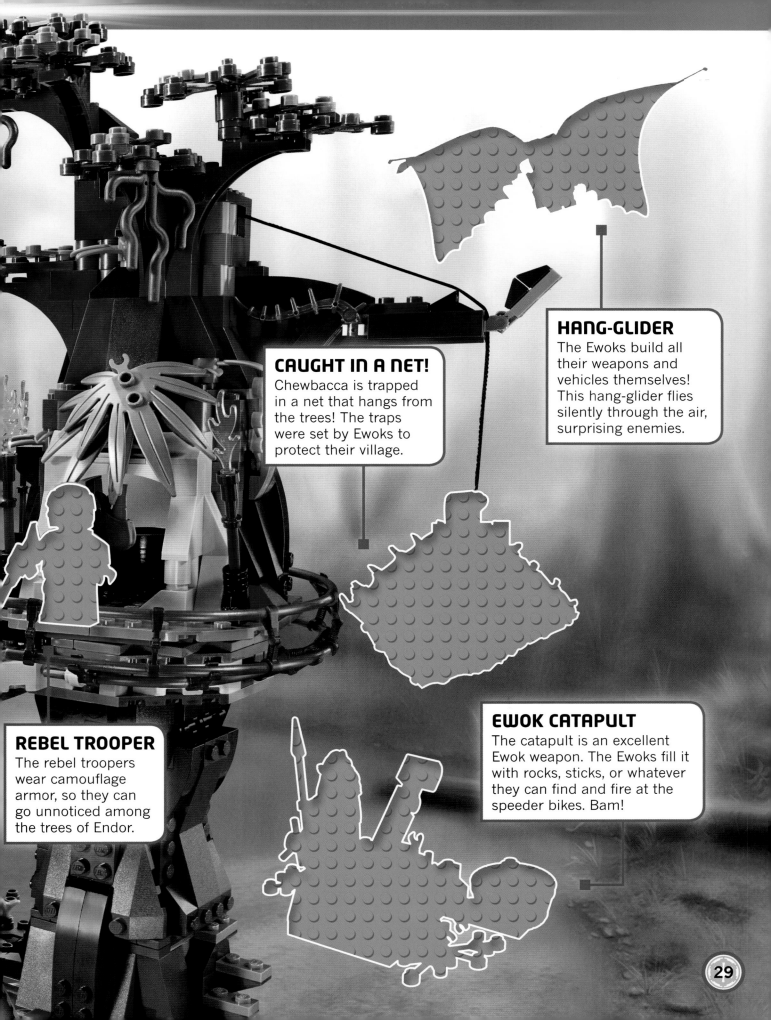

HANG-GLIDER

The Ewoks build all their weapons and vehicles themselves! This hang-glider flies silently through the air, surprising enemies.

CAUGHT IN A NET!

Chewbacca is trapped in a net that hangs from the trees! The traps were set by Ewoks to protect their village.

REBEL TROOPER

The rebel troopers wear camouflage armor, so they can go unnoticed among the trees of Endor.

EWOK CATAPULT

The catapult is an excellent Ewok weapon. The Ewoks fill it with rocks, sticks, or whatever they can find and fire at the speeder bikes. Bam!

BATTLE OF ENDOR

The Empire has built a second deadly Death Star! The rebels want to destroy it, so they can defeat the Empire once and for all. But the Death Star is protected by the Imperial fleet. Can the rebels destroy the Death Star with their fleet of small ships? The fate of the galaxy will be decided by this space battle.

DEADLY LASER
The Death Star's laser beam can destroy an entire planet!

TIE FIGHTER
Hundreds of TIE fighters swarm out of the Death Star and begin firing their laser cannons. Can the rebels dodge them?

A-WING
The A-wing is one of the fastest starships in the galaxy. It flies swiftly, avoiding the Imperial TIE fighters.

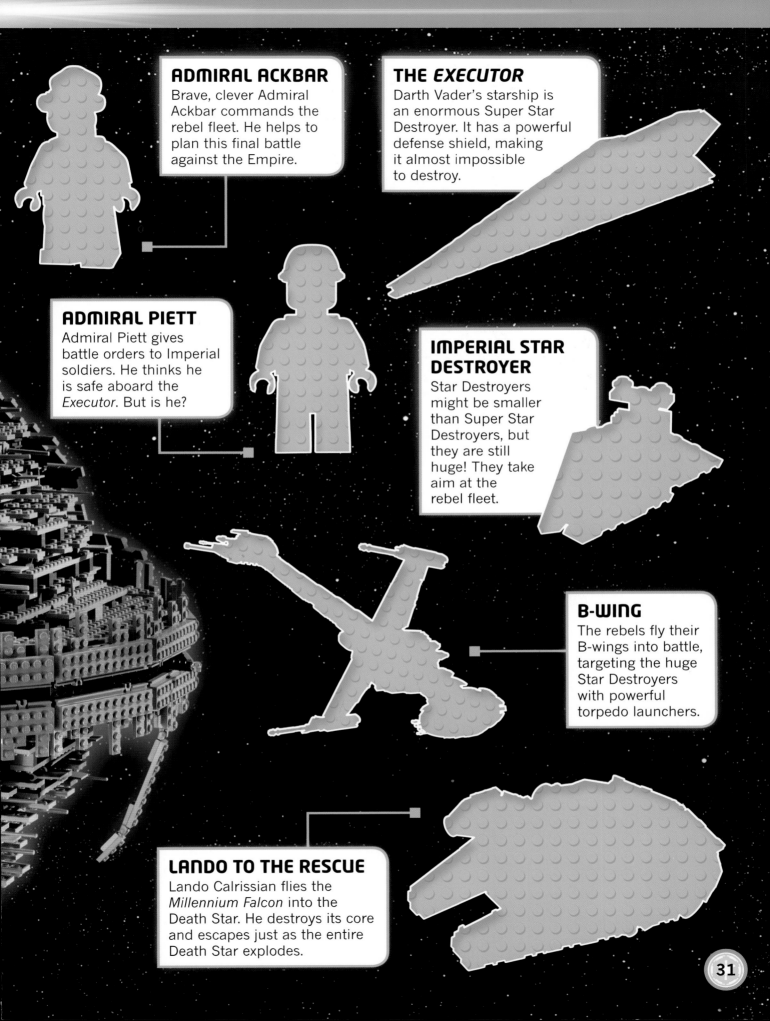

ADMIRAL ACKBAR
Brave, clever Admiral Ackbar commands the rebel fleet. He helps to plan this final battle against the Empire.

THE *EXECUTOR*
Darth Vader's starship is an enormous Super Star Destroyer. It has a powerful defense shield, making it almost impossible to destroy.

ADMIRAL PIETT
Admiral Piett gives battle orders to Imperial soldiers. He thinks he is safe aboard the *Executor*. But is he?

IMPERIAL STAR DESTROYER
Star Destroyers might be smaller than Super Star Destroyers, but they are still huge! They take aim at the rebel fleet.

B-WING
The rebels fly their B-wings into battle, targeting the huge Star Destroyers with powerful torpedo launchers.

LANDO TO THE RESCUE
Lando Calrissian flies the *Millennium Falcon* into the Death Star. He destroys its core and escapes just as the entire Death Star explodes.

BATTLESHIPS

The Imperial and rebel fleets have to consider many things before building or selecting their starships. Size, firepower, maneuverability, and speed are all important. But different ships have different strengths. Which starfighters are the best for a deadly space battle?

TIE INTERCEPTOR

These arrowlike starfighters are perfect for a fierce space battle. They are fast and maneuverable because of their small size.

X-WING

X-wings are bigger than TIE Interceptors, but they are still extremely fast. They also have a lot of firepower and a strong defense system.

IMPERIAL SHUTTLE

This luxurious ship transports Emperor Palpatine across the galaxy in safety.

CARGO SHIP

The *Millennium Falcon* is a cargo ship. It is not built for war, although it has been involved in many. Despite its large size, it is very fast and easy to maneuver.

STAR DESTROYER

Star Destroyers are huge Imperial starships. They have an enormous amount of firepower, but they are slow and clumsy during a space battle.

Nightspeeder

Octuptarra
Tri-Droid

©2014 LEGO

Battle Droid

Chief Tarfful

©2014 LEGO

Swoop Bike

Deadly
Droid

Yoda

Chancellor

Republic Attack
Cruiser

Mechanical
Legs

Palpatine

Hailfire Droid

Padmé

Jedi
Anakin

41st Elite Trooper

Stass Allie

Kenobi Vs.
Grievous

©2014 LEGO

©2014 LEGO

Apprentices
©2014 LEGO

AT-RT
©2014 LEGO

Droid Gunship
©2014 LEGO

©2014 LEGO

Capital Planet
©2014 LEGO

Jar Jar Binks
©2014 LEGO

©2014 LEGO

Commando Droid Captain
©2014 LEGO

©2014 LEGO

Alliance Tank Droid
©2014 LEGO

Count Dooku
©2014 LEGO

Plo Koon
©2014 LEGO

Separatist Droid

Obi-Wan Kenobi
©2014 LEGO

Naboo Starfighter
©2014 LEGO

Droid Tri-Fighter
©2014 LEGO

Jek-14
©2014 LEGO

Turbo Tank
©2014 LEGO

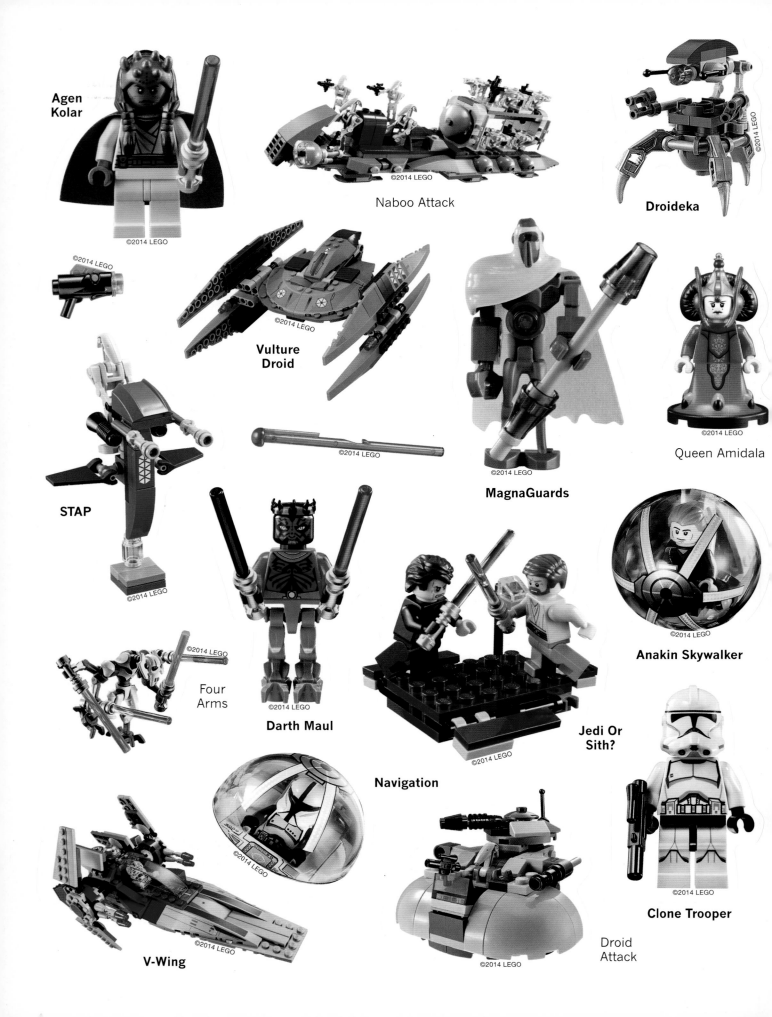

Agen
Kolar

Naboo Attack

Droideka

©2014 LEGO

Vulture
Droid

MagnaGuards

Queen Amidala

STAP

Darth Maul

Four
Arms

Navigation

Jedi Or
Sith?

Anakin Skywalker

Clone Trooper

V-Wing

Droid
Attack

Jedi Generals

Buzz Droid

Mobile Heavy Cannon

AT-TE

Sith Lightning

212th Clone Trooper

R2-A3

C-3PO

Dooku's Speeder

Utapau Troopers

Kamino

Coleman Trebor

Kashyyyk Troopers

BARC Speeder

V-Wing Pilot

Flying Droid

Space Machine

Republic
Police Gunship

AAT

General Kenobi

©2014 LEGO

©2014 LEGO

©2014 LEGO

©2014 LEGO

Rise Of A Sith Lord

©2014 LEGO

Gungan Submarine

©2014 LEGO

AT-AP

©2014 LEGO

Asajj
Ventress

©2014 LEGO

©2014 LEGO

Homing Spider Droid

©2014 LEGO

Darth Sidious

Commander
Cody

©2014 LEGO

Vulture

©2014 LEGO

Anti-Vehicle
Cannon

©2014 LEGO

©2014 LEGO

Mace
Windu

©2014 LEGO

Naboo

©2014 LEGO

Wookiee
Power

©2014 LEGO

Shock Trooper

Fighting Padmé

Saleucami Trooper

Pong Krell

Chewbacca

Saesee Tiin

Super Battle Droid

Poggle

Clone Captain

Geonosis Trooper

41st Trooper

Jedi Interceptor

R4-GO

Commander Gree

Umbaran Soldier

MTT

Command Station

Pilot Anakin

Jedi Shuttle

Catamaran

Wolfpack
Trooper

Boga

Pilotless

501st Legion
Trooper

Gungan
Soldier

Saleucami Cannon

Green
Clone

Trooper

Rocket
Battle Droid

Jedi
Gunship

Astromech Droid

Saleucami
Clone

Wheel Bike

The Jedi

Naboo
Submarine

R2-D2

Echo Base Attack

Darth Vader

Stormtrooper

Han In Danger

P-Tower Turret

Y-Wing

TIE Fighter

Hoth

Logray

Jabba's Court

Admiral Piett

Dewback

Sith Guard

Luke Skywalker

Death Star Trooper

Millennium Falcon

Max Rebo

Rebel Starfighter

Pilot Vader

Jabba's Rancor

Han On Hoth

Luke's Droid

Mon Mothma

Battle Station

R5-J2

Wicket

Droid Slave

A-Wing

Ewok

Ben Kenobi

Ewoks And C-3PO

Leia On Endor

GNK Droid

©2014 LEGO

Cargo Ship

©2014 LEGO

Rebel Trooper

©2014 LEGO

Hoth Rebel

©2014 LEGO

Princess Leia

©2014 LEGO

Droid

©2014 LEGO

Jedi Pilot

©2014 LEGO

Sandcrawler

©2014 LEGO

Death Star Gunner

©2014 LEGO

Scout Trooper

©2014 LEGO

Enemy Machine

©2014 LEGO

Probe Droid

©2014 LEGO

Lando Calrissian

©2014 LEGO

Emperor's Ship

©2014 LEGO

Endor

©2014 LEGO

Wookiee Prisoner

©2014 LEGO

Snowtroopers

©2014 LEGO

Jabba The Hutt

Brave Wookiee

©2014 LEGO

Jedi Prisoner

Vader's Starship

Han Solo

AT-AT Driver

Star Destroyer

Boba Fett

Chewbacca Takes Control!

Rebel

Leader Leia

Coruscant

General Veers

Imperial Star Destroyer

AT-AT Walker

Sith Trooper

Hoth Bunker

Jawa

©2014 LEGO

Tatooine

Oola

X-Wing

Briefing
Room

Hang-Glider

Imperial Officer

Wampa

Jabba's Band

Tauntaun

**Stormtrooper
Luke**

R5-A7

Rotta

**Ewok
Catapult**

Salacious
Crumb

**Lando To
The Rescue**

**Admiral
Ackbar**

Battle
Weapon

©2014 LEGO

Han In Carbonite

Jedi Cruiser

General Rieekan

Death Star Cannon

Snowspeeder

Leia

Rebel Han

B-Wing

Caught by Ewoks

Lando The Guard

Ewok Chief

Old Ben Kenobi

Imperial Pilot

Jabba's Sail Barge

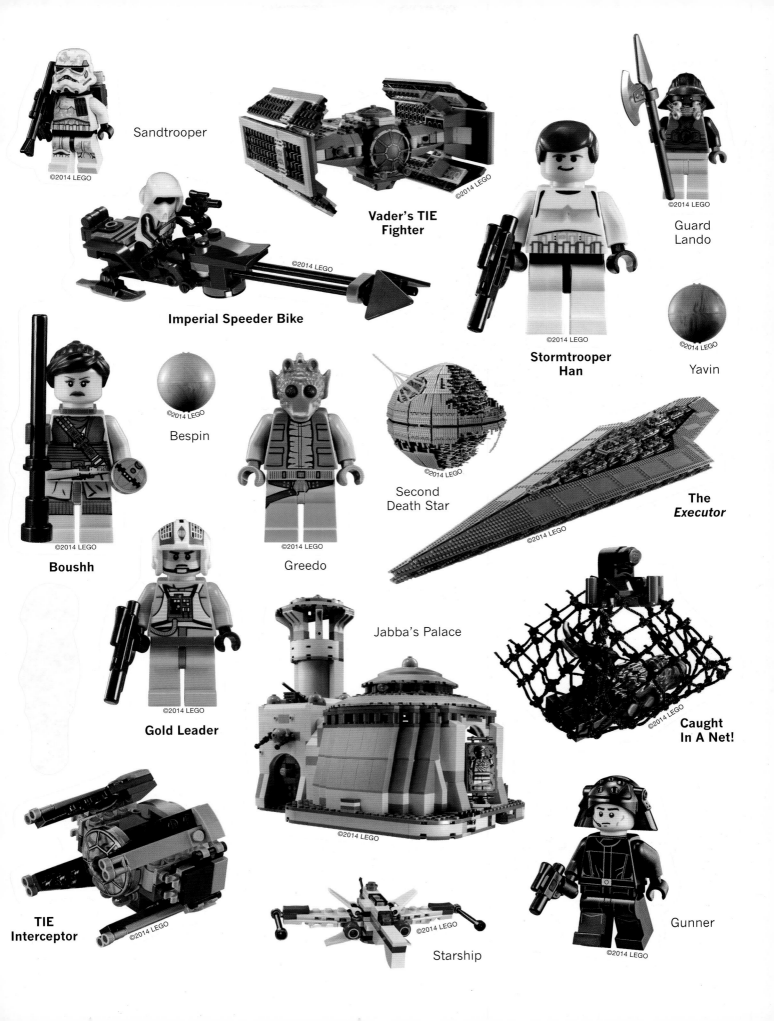

Sandtrooper

Vader's TIE Fighter

Imperial Speeder Bike

Guard Lando

Stormtrooper Han

Yavin

Boushh

Bespin

Greedo

Second Death Star

The *Executor*

Gold Leader

Jabba's Palace

Caught In A Net!

TIE Interceptor

Starship

Gunner

©2014 LEGO

©2014 LEGO ©2014 Lucasfilm Ltd.™

EXTRA STICKERS

©2014 LEGO
©2014 LEGO
©2014 LEGO
©2014 LEGO
©2014 LEGO
©2014 LEGO
©2014 LEGO
©2014 LEGO
© 2014 LEGO
©2014 LEGO
©2014 LEGO
©2014 LEGO
©2014 LEGO
©2014 LEGO
©2014 LEGO
©2014 LEGO
©2014 LEGO
©2014 LEGO
©2014 LEGO

EXTRA STICKERS

©2014 LEGO
©2014 LEGO
©2014 LEGO
©2014 LEGO
©2014 LEGO
©2014 LEGO
©2014 LEGO
©2014 LEGO
©2014 LEGO
©2014 LEGO
©2014 LEGO
©2014 LEGO
©2014 LEGO
©2014 LEGO
©2014 LEGO
©2014 LEGO
©2014 LEGO
©2014 LEGO

EXTRA STICKERS

©2014 LEGO

EXTRA STICKERS

©2014 LEGO

EXTRA STICKERS

©2014 LEGO

EXTRA STICKERS

©2014 LEGO

EXTRA STICKERS

EXTRA STICKERS

©2014 LEGO

EXTRA STICKERS

©2014 LEGO

EXTRA STICKERS

©2014 LEGO

EXTRA STICKERS

EXTRA STICKERS

©2014 LEGO

EXTRA STICKERS

©2014 LEGO

EXTRA STICKERS

©2014 LEGO

EXTRA STICKERS

EXTRA STICKERS